Counting the Days

Counting the Days

Recovery Through the Romance Side of the Brain

Tyler Stanley

iUniverse, Inc.

New York   Bloomington

Counting the Days
Recovery Through the Romance Side of the Brain

iUniverse books may be ordered through booksellers or by contacting:

iUniverse
1663 Liberty Drive
Bloomington, IN 47403
www.iuniverse.com
1-800-Authors (1-800-288-4677)

ISBN: 978-0-595-48250-4 (pbk)
ISBN: 978-0-595-60338-1 (ebk)

Printed in the United States of America

iUniverse rev. 11/25/2008

I.

Introduction

The Story

After I learned again to walk and talk I broke windows, frustrated because words wouldn't dislodge from my fractured brain. I put my fist through any type of glass, including a tough-to-break telephone booth. But my memory is weak on these points, even with my emotionally-challenged discovery of drawings and poetry, which I apparently had dictated to someone else long ago as evidenced by my words written in an unknown legible hand. I don't recognize numerous scribbles of thin suggestions scrawled across aged paper. Eventually I wrote my own poems, beginning in an immature block awkward print. I was lost inside my drawings, as the one above, being deathly focused on each intricate detail. A leaf, tree bark, a flower or a blade of grass was how I sailed away from my pain. Years later, medical evaluations measured my academic performance level around fourth grade. I was twenty-seven then. I found myself also dealing with a common result of Traumatic Brain Injury, that of anger, which is a cause of incarceration, broken families, domestic abuse or an increase in public violence. Like many others suffering with Traumatic Brain Injury, anger is both our savior and curse, one arrives with bells on to chase our heads with bolts of energy such as motivation, false courage, and determination, while the other offers an explosive additive to fuel a weakened neurologic system. With the bridge washed out and streetlights gone with a zap, anger delivered more salt in the wound, which pain led to dying. One memory of how anger sped me along a path of death felt like an artery burst at one hundred miles per hour riding flat-lined on my Yamaha RD 400, which was akin to straddling a stick of dynamite; I was the match! This tenacious effort to drive

"TBI" out of my life failed by my living, couldn't kill it without killing me. Matter-a-fact, I kept living so there's something to that. You keep living too! Once a Highway Patrol Officer pulled me over on my motorcycle near the University of California, Santa Barbara. Upon orders, I tried to remove my helmet but it was stuck like a cord in a tight socket. Pulling the helmet off finally released a long mane of blonde hair. In the dark stood an obedient-to-the-authority, lanky butch. He stared a minute, then broke into song, "Oh my God you're a girl! Oh my God. What are you doing riding like that? I have a daughter your age!" He shrieked upon seeing his first butch, defined then as those women who ride motorcycles bravely tipping fate at higher speeds. Upon a milder voice, of course, he expected a guy. "Guys are stupid and suicidal, not girls." He obviously didn't know any brain damaged ones! I stood silent taking my carving to the core like a tough "boy," wondering what was next. Arrest? I thought to myself, I had something to kill inside, My loss of life; My pain; My rage; My disorientation; My future; My dreams, that another would live not me! My mind turned back to what he was saying, still standing at attention, is that he cared! That two-stroke motorcycle was my instrument of expression and I did have a lot to say!

After the car accident my father and two older brothers left us like trash thrown out a car window, to be blown away quietly alongside a highway, or if lucky, we'd survive the repeated run-overs. My mother and I formed a bond, surviving repeated run-overs struggling through our lives minus a father's child support or alimony. We lived in poverty. The car accident that brought hell on the wind happened July 7th on Highway 46, a desolate and dehydrated country road made famous in 1955 by James Dean's tragic death in a car crash with his mechanic Rolf surviving. Like Dean's fate, someone died in my crash. I was thrown out of a roadster onto the highway at high speeds, directly on my head. I was seventeen years old then and I will never know now who I would have been, but for the accident. Nor will Rodney's parents know whether their son would've ever changed his life from where it was going with drugs at the time, because I took that. I was the driver who survived! That haunts me at my emotional center, it is hidden in everything I am. Where enormous guilt pushes my hand to scribbling poetry, to rid the angst punching against my insides, banging outward to express hell. It was the beauty of poetry written by others that drew me back to living. It was the area of my brain that stayed intact for the journey home. Where pain and sorrow could romp and spill freely from a split-gut. Where I could feel love and romance made-up, fantasized, unreal. Pen to paper over my senses of being alive. Quivering, beneath the surface buzzing through the silence of redwood trees on a sunny day. I was living. I created a world I could bear to acknowledge through poetry. A world, in which I would recover my self, not the dark hole thought to be me. A remanufactured self, but nonetheless a person, to eventually find great love and passion transformed through literature.

Poetry penetrated a brain that no longer sensed or connected with "real" pain. As a reminder, I'd put cigarettes out on the back of my hand. Done during recess in the yard mingling with other locked-up psych ward crazies. Yes there are scars. But I never winced. I didn't feel pain. I felt poetry. When I watched my skin smoke it was no more upsetting then the news of the day. Burning my flesh, I imagined a glowing dot pulling me in. A lava-colored transparent red windowpane opened to my soul, just smoldering. Then one day, I jumped back from burning, the practice was over. I not only didn't want pain, but I could feel it as the cigarette came within closer proximity. I was a miserable heap of someone who had no past, no present, and certainly no future. I was the question mark!

Yet, poetry reached me, keeping me from falling through the red-stained window. Love and romance fed my desire to feel anything good about living. As if "future" were an item one could win or buy from surviving battle like a powerful winged, flying dragon swooping over the forest, or the mightiest sword pulled from the stone waiting years for its master's strength. I would discover through monumental pain and suffering, a steady private romancing of my soul. The heart center of my brain romantically revived my body, shuttering it to the living. "Something" feeling painfully good, that could hold my feet to the ground while propelling me upward, to climb hope's highest mountain as the writer and poet emerged. The broken comes to the page with desperate dreams in hand.

After my accident my brain was completely disconnected like a severed ventricle, the ends sanded clean of any association of the other before seventeen. In the last photo of me, I am standing in front of a wire fence in a public park. I look at the photo now to see a young girl, one who died suddenly in a crash. That one I don't know? My childhood recollections are spotty where memories are held in conflict. It is the remake of any great movie. The script begins at the computer screen, blank of course. If you are reading this book you are part of my dream so welcome to my succeeding against trauma that devoured years of my life. This work is for those who faithfully survive life's crippling effects of disability. It is for those of us who dare to scale hope's mountain while broken, to kneel before her majestic heights unafraid. One step at a time keeps your eye on the peak!

II.

Acknowledgements

A book doesn't grow on its own without roots to provide its nutrition, or spring from cold, dark, nothing going on outside infinity without careful design. We are who we share our lives with as if our reflections. My nutrition drew from the following nutrients: Jan who watered the growth of this book by making it appear out of solid bedrock! That rock is me! She further provided a safe crevasse by making late night fires for warmth with her kids Zorro and Abbey, opinioned tails twitching and wagging, as my most dedicated writing team. Jan infused a wilted confidence with bursts of bright encouragement for this Writer to find her wings! She attended hot days at the Santa Rosa Book Festival, once to cool we ran through a fountain before leaving town. She read draft after draft tired, and when I saw her tears, it meant I had hit my target. In the second chapter, she is responsible for the photographic story of our uniquely special relationship. I fly beyond with a writer's voice because of the years loving her. To Mike and Erika for their friendship and the lovely "Belveron" cocktail now made in Texas! Good grief! Can you two do something about that? To dearest Gerard, who provides me a deeply, uniquely-trusted friendship, and without his professional advertising genius and photo talents, my business cards, etc., would be lost. To Rochelle, who like me seeks a like-minded heart to cultivate passionately on the back roads with the top down on a hot day. She's provided me so much including the gift of a fabulous APPLE computer, to complete this dream project. To my mother who gave constantly, and tirelessly, her committed advocacy, which perseverance turned a hopelessly disabled victim into a tall survivor! With her fists pointed sharply at the buzzards who were mostly those working in the social services field, she fought them at a time when I could not fend for myself. I too easy the prey, flailing in the dangers against their repeated uncaring and incompetence. Thanks to Ventura College's Student Disabilities Program that shielded me against daily harms, being so vulnerable. There I found safety and began the journey to heal my brain. Learning on an APPLE computer made any level of success possible, being the only computer operating system smart enough to teach a damaged brain how to win! To Jill Winter who long ago kept me out of a mental institution, insisting I wasn't crazy, but injured. To Janny M., who believed in my drawings, which appear in the first chapter. And to so many more people who have come through my life to make this the little book that could!

III.

Dedication

To our intended lovers whose hearts break while dying for our touch, and to, of course, the survivor who lives to love, hearing the recovery side of the brain's music!

IV.

Table of Contents

Chapter 1

Unknown - 2000

"When I Feel Trapped I'll Write Myself Out" Victim of Traumatic Brain Injury

Chapter 2

2000-2008

The Recent Years

"The Survivor Emerged"

Chapter 1

Unknown - 2000

"When I Feel Trapped I'll Write Myself Out"
Victim of Traumatic Brain Injury

1.

BALLAD OF AN IMAGINED WOMON

I'll try love again even after
this
'cause I haven't found you
yet.
I thought I might've
stumbled into the dream,
but so soon it became
nothing more,
nothing less,
than the rest,
in a past of wandering.

Your mouth I imagine,
your walk I praise.
Gentle softness *womon unlaid*,
tender giver of shy ways.

You pull at my sleep
keep me from sadness
'cause I imagine you're coming here.
So tired of wasting my time.
So many lines to filter through,
not enough truth,
just lies.

Tired, so tired tonight.

How much longer will you tease my need?
Do you feel me bleed?
you're thinking to meet me
around any corner
down a crowded street.
I wait for your face to appear,
your arms to take hold.
Kiss and tell me you're not gonna' leave.
Stay with me-----stay,
though it just be in my sleep.
I'll know when you reach me
I'll know when you call,
given to madness so I've been told,
standing naked,
knowing,
thinking,
We've shared a common dream.
Touching my lips to your breast
and within your *pure*, I rest my head.

2.

AMBER'S CORN

Streets of fire
running bare on hot red coals
radiation of heart
when the fire turns up.

Life in flames
the future's burning
inside my window.

Ash is not golden, nor sweet to eat
fires blaze as mine eyes set far through--
time is burning,
dreams dwindle to ashen haze
I gaze to participate.

A farmer churns the dirt
she's digging; she's digging,
mad.
Soul for the banquet
sweat trickles then storms
harm besiege the pores of her skin
those who dared.
Waste trying buried forgotten
fires blaze when the heat's turned up
forgotten on the stove.

Sparse fields of green digested
scarcity arrives wherein emotional collapse,
the death of dirty faces and lost articles of what grew
not properly tended by you.

Bare running on hot coals leaping for a clear
a tender spot there,
her dreams become water light like feathers taking off
a break in the weather
eyes heavy believe
dousing flames.

A seed is left standing
no tear.
And there is no shame to be trying,
hard work and planting is it!
Sprouting proudly in her dirt
strengthened like tinsel, taut and true.
Bow and string conjoin sweetly
music instinctively breaks into a hum upon daybreak
alone in the field, the warm winds rise.

Heart grows strong in the green
life gets its start again
freedom is the only breath upon to wait.

Corn howls to the sun,
a *seed* has come!
Sprung up
new day,
one without rain, fire or pain.
While hope, not further from my anguished mind
is the 'morrow of birth squeezed of her yesterday.
Once of an endless pain a perceived death.
A lack of faith to bust the thing
Suddenly.

3.

LYING ON BONES

Dust to hardness
hardness to the *cut*
chopped, ground and peeled
to the bone
spit in the eye,
shift of weight,
the eye spit me.
Difference to die for unknown
envy said to be.

SHARE A SUNNY DAY WITH A FRIEND, AND A LITTLE SPACE!

Dust and spit,
life passing before my eyes
my structure pained upon the heap
like blue paling
the color of death
the color of life,
standing on ends below ground.

I wish for all,
I hope for nothing,
Bones.
Dust.
Reframe my carcass
in your name
of freedom
where all are joined,
not only two,
or certain ones,
on a wave or soaring to one.

Wishes fall dead
dreams laugh at you
nothing but bone
Turn to dust.
To carcass
no more a wandering eye
shining on you,
no longer the frame of a person once I knew,
gone to dust.

4.

VERONICA

A typewriter
from a second-hand store,
the writer lives no more.
A mental trail in the air
and the scent of writer's ink
once a grand illusion.

My words aren't for sale
I'm not so insecure,
just want to share
What I think *of*
a grand illusion.

Like the panther isn't really pink
she's just a child's link
to Saturday afternoon.
She tells the time, by cartoon.

5.

LETTER

Only yesterday you told me
the ocean was beautiful
the sun would always shine
why so fast
did you change your mind?
Wasn't worth your time.
Your heart turned to stone
in the middle of the night
while lying by my side.
If I had known,
I would have woke you up.

I write your name in the sand
next morning,
speak your name among friends
in the mirror pretending you
read old letters,
renew my tears,
and hear reality.
You're gone, never to return,
it couldn't have been all lies
just a game
you must be hurt too.
I'm sorry for us
I wanted to make it,
you couldn't see
I faded.
Of who you needed.

6.

BEAUTY

I've always had this vision
of what my life will bring.
Success, money,
a beautiful house in the mountains
wood and glass
green trees all around
soil touched by morning rain,

a jet black Carrera
fast enough to leave all behind.
Something is missing
wonder why?
Stereo loud while flying
phone for calling longer distance.

As I pull up to my house
smell the scent of morning past
of wood and glass,
all I wanted was love first
an easy run up the viable stairs,
pour a glass of French wine.

Sit in the huge chair swallowed up.
Suddenly I know,
I'm alone.
I've been relentless for years to succeed.

Strained tears fall into wine,
sometime I could have touched ground,
fear brought me here.
Those tears.
Why couldn't I change
when I had you here?

A toast to what it could have been,
a toast to what it isn't at all,
too late now

at 165,
the road is shorter by the mile
as I run beauty off this cliff
to touch ground.

7.

QUEST

Oh please *spiritual* lord
grant my plea for validation,
as few understand me
I look into the forest
I look into the sea
Crazy making.
Standing amid the earth's brow
on edge,
on edge.
I surrender my troubled soul to thee
amongst thickening trees
blinded.
Thy promises reflected
behind the red door evil or good?
Spring box of sun contained tightly,
watered without care by duty.
I cry no tears today,
dry and brittle to the slightest sound
breakdown.

Time passed already stretched
showing worn.
I know no more than yesterday
quest,
does prayer go away when I die?
Does hope replace?
Burdened to oppressed dark thoughts,
I carry the rock.
Depleted of faith
despair,
landing.
You've said a gift upon my next good deed,
I humble myself before *thy* wit and humor.
This pain is 'tine!
Laughing.
Tis' too heavy
breathing.

8.

WHISKEY CHANGE

I wrote a good piece
while living in the streets
I put it in my pocket
it's tucked away in my jeans,
whiskey words.

When I die it won't be
on satin sheets
but on the dirty city streets
where I wrote a good piece.

To look at me
you'd say I was the one to lose
no longer you remember it's you,
what I see in the city.

All I need is some change
would you like to buy a few words?
Just might be the thing to use
when it's you.

9.

AS THE SHADOW

As the shadow wilts
onto these liquidated pages
reflecting goddess
through a window glass.
Your tears fall of a cause,
sun cast her light
calling reflection,
finds dark traveling the past of unpredicted,
in wandering through,
any night,
any night,
is like my future.
Dark, then light and hopeful,
torrent
With no destination said or reciprocated,
but through conscience
into a dream,
make me something before I *die,*
making it somewhere
before it ends!

10.

MOUNTAIN PARADISE

I haven't loved you like I can
caught inside a picture on your wall,
you don't know I am alive.

I want so much to pull you into my arms
into an old wood cabin—I painted myself,
high on a mountain meadow
hidden in the pines.
I'm the heart you hear that beats within your dreams,
the voice you hear last when you fall asleep.
Coming to love you,
to set you free with *mine.*

11.

CONVERSATION WITH SELF

Conversation needed
befallen by the pull of hell,
a black hole with the arms of love
surround.

To describe this ocean
is to never understand,
to question her power
You understand less.

To take life under
she finds no challenge
for you to resist.
You've become the sands
where tides do wander.

How is this concept,
that we know none
not enough,
and to ponder nothing a lot
to drown again
willingly
to give heart knowingly.

Always waiting on
someone to care
for a short time
thought she was there,
not to know the wind from the sea
fool.
If perhaps it passed through, it was not mine.

It's always been from a distance
I've seen
those feelings
overcome,
what I've learned to believe
changes as they occur like waves come,
what is?

12.

ON WHILE

The winds pass hurriedly through
winter,
the imprint of cold and restlessness
soul stretched cold,

time call another season this night
of sun,
warmth,
of light.

I remain wanting of you
who I cannot reach,
distance is grand
not strangers
before we met,
life is possessed by possibility
riding on,
beyond comprehension of you,
sleep,
to call upon a dream.

Moments of you give me pleasure
years gone and past,
I am still but caught
I shall not die
I bear no age
remain the same,
only seasons change
outside my window.

13.

NORTH COAST

I feel the need to walk a shore
to feel the sands beneath my feet,
my lips to taste the salt and mist simultaneously,
Northern Coast
calls upon me.
Cambria on my way
moonstones collected upon wishes
no place as this sea,
so many pieces
scattered about,

a storm from a mile's distance
darkens my view,
chills my life through
tears spill from my eyes
standing upon the rocks while I cry.
I recall the day
I touched you inside
just a short time past it would seem,
I died.
I could fall from this, I scream,
I could climb above
letting tears release my entire life in a swell.
Oh how she wins, I cry,
she runs through the odds that bind most
touching,
taste the sand you kneel upon now in deep
a pause in the rain
it's me, I think.
Do you remember just how we kissed?
With emotion of leaves scattering
birds fluttering
reaching heat,
the sun folds
now gather these pieces
fragments recall who was then whole,
love
feeling gone
to all I am
to all I will be
returning here,
to the sea
to recall
to capture
you here again,
kissing salt
dreaming on feeling
I'm driving hard
to never leave this ocean inside.

14.

WHAT TO DO WITH THOSE LOVING PIECES

It is still that you don't understand
something like years gone,
I've been spilling years on waiting
for the loss of you
dreaming,
dreaming much harder now
you'll appear unexpectedly
I'm here,
It's so very strange
we loved each other so much,
we pushed it away
too hard to handle
too young to stay.

But womon,
three hundred miles,
I feel you inside my night
pushing me out of my mind,
soft kisses to change my blue
into my heart,
It'll always be you
stabbing,

It is still that you don't understand,
I look at roses
palm of my hand,
how it was once clearer
going to be you,
sad songs begin to play
I sorrow.
The stormy sky
I recall our love
so strong,
so fine,
we moved
a laugh,
a whisper I love you
I can't lie with another
carved sand all I remember
so empty
without your hands
inside mine,
can you feel this? It's what I know
walking alone.

PAT STANLEY
ODEION CENTRE OF ART
AND LEARNING.

15.

WINGS

Taking off into your vision
counting on clouds and rainbows
to paint your scene,
you're set at the odds of reality
ink and wash sketches of suffering,
leading you down the same road twice
still not getting it right,
take off into your dream
freedom in flight,
a desperate magic
released.

You're better at life
when possessed by fantasy
let onto yourself,
become wings.

16.

APPLY HEARTACHE

Love's a stake
in the earth,
producing life all along.
We're all needed here,

for what we have to hide,
hide who we are,
apply heartache to your list
of what we do.

Being like you
if you'll see through

your own,
your own disparate magic,

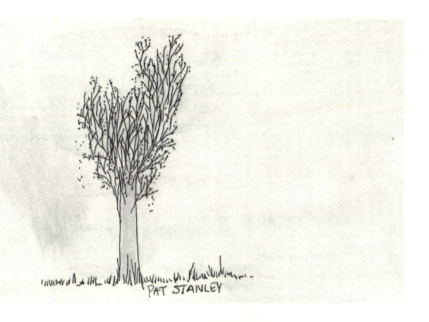

a product of what you hear
not always what's been said,
I'm not as you seem
don't cast me down
love's a stake
in the earth,
producing life all along.
We're all needed here. Love's a stake
if in solid ground
it won't wash away,
if it should rain.
(In the name of forever
Don't give *me* up)

17.

PAPER AIRPLANES

Life's got to be
the worst race of all,
just when you've got a win
you fall.
Depression,
war,
and breaking hearts.
How long can you hang on?

Searching all your life
for who you really are
and when you die
someone cries
about what they lost.

The sadness in the world
reflects the quality of minds
can't stand a world so blind.

Like a star
I try to reach the darkness
in the sky to light,
and when you die
someone cries
about what they lost
again.

18.

GUNNING FOR LIFE!

What am I going to do with a dream?
It's a lie,
just a lie I tell myself
in the middle of a night
when I can't sleep.

I challenge my mind
to a game of suicide,
and a dream did pass before my eyes
and saved my life
one time.
There was a reason to live on this life.

What is your reason?
Do you have a dream like mine?
Is it love that keeps you moving?
Or do you ever think of time?

Do we only know of failure?
And only dream to succeed?
Just a lie we tell ourselves,
to stay alive so to slide by.

19.

THEN JANNY

To face now
it's you I've also lost
would be to take on
more than my strength can defend.
I must now see that I must lie to my heart
as not to fall apart,
to pretend a future for us to share
that no other will hold you
in passion
before I shall win.
A blade of grass will rise from fired fields burned to ash
so shall I return,
something enough for you to love
with you as my desire,
I shall not stop.

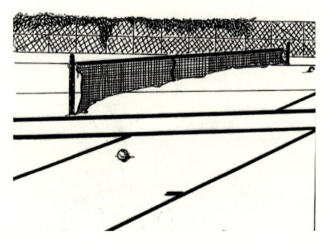

As yet nothing,
I am to give.

20.

CARIBOU

Are you ever going to love someone?
or will there be
someone always in love with you?
….In a rush to know.

Like water comes and goes
never ending in a continual flow
like winter's Eastern falling
no chance to reach you then,
You're too cold.

Intense like fire,
your desire to be loved,
a fear burns much stronger to lead you off.

21.

SATURDAY'S BROKEN WRITER

Not another word,
hide your thoughts inside
a prophet dies
in the middle of
a new word
or a profound idea
Anonymously.

22.

PROCESS

Just one more good-bye
and I'll leave your life,
just hear my feeling through,
I'm in love with you.
Didn't know before,
it has been so hard for me to speak the words that are so deep,
un-arranged, not practiced or said,
so afraid
to trust,
feelings not tried before
so unprepared for love.
Won't you wait?

23.

THOSE DRAGONS ARE REALLY CLOUDS

I hold in my palm
what used to be a *dream*,
I could feel,
I could see,
where the road could be leading me
so I stayed on.

Journey aside
constant defeat
tighter and tighter
I squeezed.
Trying to believe in me
through the times,
it slipped away
wanting to *die*
but stood again,
shaking my hand
mad at this dream

turning on me,
it just has't to be!
Tears I shed
in a constant fight
laid awake
in the night,
that life is mine,
blessed it's not,
this life is mine.

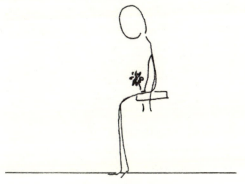

Scary in the sky,
if I could settle for less
my spirit should finally, finally rest.

24.

GUSTINE

My silence is my only road
so far traveled headed home,
in a night.
Where I sit upon the stone
to ponder life's wave
upon time.

25.

CIRCUS WIRE

Standing on a circus wire
hanging on by desire
with nothing to prove
in the arms of you.

Not a frantic *façade*
in order to please,
being with you
is being me.

Hell's not my fire
nor my future to bear,
standing on a circus wire
hanging on by desire.

Love feels good
letting you in
it's worth the heartache,
in the end.
With nothing underneath,
to ease my fall.
I shake in my dreams,
but when waking up with you
I fall off to sleep,
satisfied.
In the arms of love
holding onto me.

26.

GEMINI WOMON

It's hard to be you
you're really two,
one side wants to stay
the other has packed her things,
left them near the door.

War within.
It's hard to be you
you're really two,
careless and impulsive
restrained at times,
chosen for the leader
just when your weak side shows.

It's hard to be you
you're really two,
still hear every word.
As your eyes dart around the room
taking in the psychology of the place
rather a debate about an important topic,
than making love – sometimes.
Seems a waste of intellectual minutes,
physical indeed.

It's hard to be you
invited to all the parties
for your boundless entertainment.
All the womyn want you
a challenge you are.
Try to hold you down – you want to get up.

27.

DAWNING

I don't want you here
you are my ache.
I don't want you here
you interfere,
with what I need,
leave.
My needs aren't met with you near
please dear go.
Find another day to play another fool,
I'm better off
I know this now
with my mind on something else,
like moving forward.

28.

FOREVER INSIDE

I've had it now –
you've toyed with my mind
taken my time,
and abused this situation.

You said love –
I said I'd play,
that was long ago,
take a look at our lives today.
It didn't take rain,
to wash away a good feeling
it could have been lost
on a sunset or summer day.

With little help from you
to find what we had
let's let it go now,
until sunrise.

With affections tossed
to the wind
I say, with my back turned,
with me, it will never end,
It still won't change
That I must walk away.

29.

SATURDAY IN NEW ENGLAND

I felt pain when I watched you cry
I felt so helpless,
looking into your eyes
with so much grief over me.

I do believe that it's best this way
never look too fast into your past
can't move on that way.

It's a Saturday in New England
it's a Monday here in France
just a lady I knew
on a glance.

I really couldn't touch her
she wasn't you
what you believe,
or the language I speak,
are never the same, today.

30.

AN ARTIST WORKS ALONE

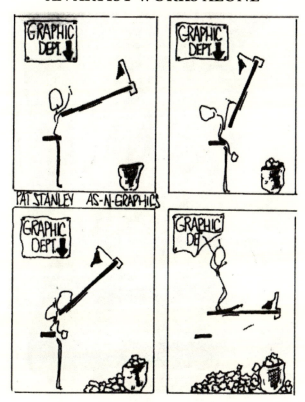

When are you going to understand?
Human behaviors are so easy to read.
You only hide from yourself
leaving the rest exposed for
everyone else.
More information than I need.
Feeling every line on the page.
Dripping wet. Agony. Cultivating.

An artist works alone.
I'm walking out again to live in my head.
Turning you off!
It's what I know.

31.

HENCE

It's where you find it.
Don't play on love's tenderness.
Lies won't win it,
not a kiss that sticks either,
yet forever will.

Looking where you
left it several times.
On society's lady,
only going to kiss for love.

Believing in imagination.
Falling into my arms.
Knowing that I wait chanting,
to catch.

I can't go wrong
for she's all that I want.
I need her,
as soon as,
this beggar's wish will carry....
By pigeon,
by floating bottle,
under pillow,
in the mail,
over the bridge
driving for miles.
It is what it is!

32.

BROKEN UP

I will stay for a few more drinks
trying to recall what's been good.

33.

FORTUNE IN MY DIRECTION

Tide's getting low
Life's much too slow
ready for a run
across the beach I fly.

Fortune in my direction
wind in my face.
a good friend
just ahead.

Feel it in my hand
glance behind.
Only footprints in the sand
no one lives there any more
that place is dead.

Ready for a run
across the beach I fly.
Fortune in my direction
passing reflections,
peace.
Footprints in the sand
of someone once there.

34.

DOG EAR THE PAGE

Turning the pages of my future,
drowning my past disappointments with a spot of gin.
Love conquers where lonely lives.
A room apart from light.
A place without a smile for a passerby
cold in the cellar of life.
The center of us all turned at the end of the hall, to the right then downstairs.
Crowds don't mix with the tears rising to the top.
They bring up the volume.
Crowds make me cry.
Scared by the noise.
Then there was, putting me down in front of my family.
Shamed me in their eyes.
Thinking you were, a friend?
Look what I've realized.
Filtering like rain.

35.

E.R.A.

Only an answer for one moment
then you must decide
which way to turn,
to solve the problem.
Learn to stand for yourself.
But don't refuse to help another, don't forget what it's like
to need.
Womyn be strong for equal rights
We have to fight
to be freed.
It's independence
basic to humanity,
all should have the chance
to live as one wishes
even womyn.

36.

RUNNING OUT

Running out
going through the gears
she's flat on the road
won't slip in my tears.

A part of myself
just won't cry
she has no fears
nobody ask why.

Better than roses,
cheaper than the price of
friends.
Love can reach me.

Nothing breaks through
pedal to the floor
and I can run out
on you.

PAT STANLEY

37.

TIME'S EXPLODING

I'd like to see the sun rise
One more time.
To fix my eyes on an ocean view
and save all my days for you.

Keeping my tears inside
to release in the night
so you won't know I'd cried.

Facing the truth
doesn't mean I'm brave
maybe just a fool.
My smiles are for you.

We thought we had
every year from yesterday
and in a moment it slipped away.

38.

STAGE FRIGHT

You're older than I?
Experience won't always bring knowledge
you have to let it in.
Donavan put the sun to bed,
la de da…
Get out of your head,
for logic maybe?
Carley Simon wants to marry me on the radio.
Joni Mitchell's
a troubled child in the same situation.

Use an imagination.
Our first night explosive,
like discovering America.
Stars and stripes
aren't forever
la de da…

Unless . . . yes.
That isn't for you.
Bad Company says,
me and you together
that's not for us either.

39.

"ELO"

I'm getting out of love.
It's show time.
Oh not tonight,
'cause.

40.

TRAUMATIC BRAIN INJURY

The rain that falls, that never stops,
the collector.
Collector of dreams and of my years, harvesting me
of personhood, prolonged, and purpose,
of youth and growing on a stick.
The thief that steals your life's means and ends,
spinning against God and hope
without her intention to return you,
can't speak or drive,
think or love.
Expression shattered glass, the clear plate void in *self*,
the *armor* falling,
heaven break me?
Living scared, disabled,
wearing a coffin dressed in pine wood *shroud*,
I feel for thy hardest road,
the one that lives on never stopping to rest.
Long, and longest- you cry on your way.
I feel that pain of which you are, and know why you fear mobility.
Dance to know, not where your dreams skip lightly.
Begging right foot to Spanish tile floor,

try as you will, eat rock and harder times.
Swallow, as you would like it forced into your mouth by fists.
Tuned and ready, but a sputter,
A sputter choking on one's own blood.
How dare you believe in me!
It's the wall, the locked doors that never go,
collector of filthy gutters and failed attempts,
no launching.
The rain, constant until broken when no vision of sun will exist,
warmth slips into routine what's before is always.

41.

ICE AGE

Just give me one night,
when she feels as summer does,
her lips on mine,
I'll always stay,
locked.

You act like you just slid
off the cover of a leading magazine,
made-up to please,
sexy so… on and on,
you're such a tease,
you walk as though carried,
blown through
my heartstrings again and again.

42.

LOVE SLIP AWAY

Pat

The more you've got to hide
the stronger the drive
don't let it rule your life,
it's just a dream or a wish
for something else.
Don't let love slip away
'cause you think it will get in the way
of getting rich.
The only rare opportunity is love
and someone to trust.
It's just a dream or a wish
for something else,
more than shopping.
Don't let love slip away
to spend.

Gazing into winter's rain and snow
when I need you most,
to hold me warm from the cold.

I counted on seeing a rainbow
though someone else got the gold,
the pot was empty,
I fell through the hole.

That's the way it goes
when you're swallowed up
by your own,
I counted on you
and it's someone else you're with.
I tried.
Looking for a rainbow
in winter's grey gloom,
coldness runs through you.
I can see it in your eyes,
when you lie to rest in the night.
Your business mind is working overtime,
you're finding the world hard to bear,
the understanding isn't there,
just what you think.
Are the books you read
wanting to touch you for love?
And then you're gone.
All my heart locked in a song
to be written some day
so I can explain
what you won't hear~
heart-on.
A desire to be loved,
we haven't lived until
we've touched her,
every day she's in a change,
a need for disclosure.
Much stronger than I can give
I don't know a way to please *her*.
Oh! God don't say to leave
like *water*.
She comes and goes
in a downward commotion.
Oh! She flows,
she can feel like seasons,
an Eastern snow.
I can't reach her through the coldest winter *of* fear of trust.

Chapter 2

2000-2008

The Recent Years

"The Survivor Emerged"

43.

BABYCAKES

Danger: I put up a barricade after 30 days of your passing warning others of certain hazards such as the road is now closed!

I knew after you left the roadside diner with a hot cup of coffee steaming upwards in your hand that I was leaving this place. Watchful as the steam wound spiraling into the cool morning air my body suddenly quivered. I recall that the sun erupted from complete and permanent darkness into orange that day. I watched as you walked to your car in a short leather skirt and was drawn by the trail of steam you left behind. A Jag convertible sat in the dirt lot. I could feel something omnipresent pushing me into speaking. But I remained silent. Then I was pumping gas next door waiting until a better job came around; but in a small town one has fewer choices. I turned to look to where the pressure originated and she was me looming over my shoulder. Day was breaking like a thin shell and I was caught between two worlds, only one was real.

My eyes continued to follow your smoke, thinking— turn around and bless me with your beauty, cutie. Come take a drive with me. Be overwhelmed by the match I strike with you. Like a flower fully bloomed in summertime when you're ready. To be watered by this deep exchange. And we all can use warmth like the sun. Let me be the one to pleasure you, and you me.

Dearest, this just popped out in the wake of my resisting performing more PI work this morning. But got to leave this warm place, to reenter the hard work world. Had my break today for a moment in my world. Like to live in ours, so coming through.
Hope it gives you a smile at least.

44.

MORNING 'TINE

Come morning waking to the storm,
of moisture and heat cooking under tight seal,
simmering skin nearly ready,
smell of rain falling,
pitter-patter of Mendocino,
sweet pea's incubating land,
your eyes.

The mast where I raise my sail,
under wind of your wings,
the moment I am
all I struggle to be.
The sea, the wave that pounds me to splinters,
you, mornings.

Fear thwarted,
failure no road to drive,
no mountain to climb,
in your arms I thrive.
The clock my tormentor,
responsibility a tear flowing,
branches snapped off in cold,
life clears a path without tenderness.

But behold,
peeking near the hour,
hanging by the side to enter,
next morning,
stopping the tyrant clock, to sleep awhile,
tightly percolating under seal,
sweetness to feast,
of morning dew.
Too long between baking.

45.

VALENTINE'S, YOUR WAVE

Lover, come back.
Wherever gone?
Fence closed shut,
locked down heart.
No long winding country road after mornings,
splash.
Walking in the sun,
dogs barking.
View of skin naked outside
my intense touch upon your soft shoulder.
Blue falls off edge
from your mountain
lips rise perfectly set,
splashing the horizon,
Sweetbriar rose.
Orange sky calls to openness,
ostrich running but cannot fly.

Clouds above, dizzy carrying my tears,
not a simple thing to love,
Sweetbriar rose.
Passing away,
gone one day,
think it to stay,
be real or sure.
But upon a hurricane,
the sky goes black,
cackling light shoots yonder,
street hot, but wet.
Crying a long time,
reaching across the sheets.
Pick any star alone to wish
realizing,
dreams aren't fish,
so easy to catch,
the big one got away
in less than 730 days,
minus a month or two.
Valentine's strikes a hand for the few still,
clash of moments, not forgotten,
imprinted burned upon my system,
tattooed.

Empty promises,
that communication might've saved,
but fear gives way.
Heavy earth slides under love's weight
rains for years.
Sad and bleak
but free.
Could have worked; but for
the missing.
What should we have done?
Other than truest love,
could it be more?
Not so.
No one ever will as much as I for you,
Yet I am not enough.
You're too much.
So the tree falls blocking the road
sealing the path,
never going home,
wishing you,
Sweetbriar rose
more than I was,
next year?
After that no end.

46.

SAYING GOODBYE

Blue eyes.
Dear morning sweet smelling dew on damp skin
a touch I trusted to my demise,
kissing through the night,
I inhale you.

I'm back for another buck-off of your precious life,
thrown from the saddle of love,
sucked nectar to keep hold of the strands unraveling.
Buckles undone,
hot and subdued in nights lost.
Sweat blends like fresh baked,
upon molten moon and redwood in shade.
Silver decorates,
she stares,
I stare.
I think from afar
how few doors open anymore,
heart-work, the slave.
What it would look like to not have met you,

I do dare when tears can creep undetected,
seeing streets darker and colder than now,
but anymore than I ask.
The night is loneliness over told,
we've heard stars and listened to clouds,
I shutter,
to not live this life,
where I shared a morsel with you,
shut down for wanting so much.
Do people shut doors on love?
Miss her to my taking the knife,
yet I turn to ponder,
was it
another time?
Look upon the wind for her arrival over skylight
stars and clouds delight,
sailing over poles, and fences,
haste to reach into your front pocket.
Saddle up!
Shadow
in the dark,
I am broken she's gone.
She's pulled the rug.
Silence is her weapon.
Silence makes me yell.
Withdrawing her sheath holding to *still* blade,
cut to ribbons where pieces no longer relate,
scattered about,
flailing painfully on the street loosely named
Better get!

47.

ZORRO

My sit in life, a park bench
melting over on my back for a scratch from my mommy.
Waiting at the door wiggling upon hearing Scooter.
Waking up drowsy for a fingertip of coffee feeding like a hungry chick.
Down under the covers he goes warmly sleeps so contently.
Safe and complete upon blades of dry grass.
If this worked yesterday he says, then likely today and tomorrow too?

48.

SURVIVAL WHERE DREAMS ARE LOST

Living for working,
working to make a living,
dreams smack the wall over,
unconsciously weeping.
Hope can only do so much,
to save the soul,
the liquid pool,
I long to swim endlessly,
unattached to the must do's;
paying the rent,
buy food,
gas in the car,
affording at such a cost,
of time and dreams lost.

49.

LESBIAN POSTING

No borders.
No fences.
No barbed wire puncturing my heart.

No scratches.

No puns.

No critical jokes served cold blind.

No out of season hunting or pot shots;

No running away or skipping stones without me,

Love me or not.

Stay or go.

We aren't cookies so the middle isn't worth the wait,

no between,

stay if so.

When it's supabulous magnitudal burst of ray heat and storm let it rain do
the work and loving home,

let it go.

Sink into the beauty like flower; like sun with me alone,

unwind the Universe to be what our purpose is,

no stop signs or poor is me,

no ropes to hang,

no pissed off without reason,

no duct tape sealing around edges,

fight for love, or don't invite it in.

Be alone in the dark or satisfied.

No perfect.

No being you.

Be light.

Touching deep, to burning my bones,

then flee,

recoil in fear,

block your heart,

no curses permitted.

Commitment expected after 736 days.

Leaving emotionally won't make you free.

My heart will follow thee…

living, breathing inside your body awaking

in a mirror, in another face, in someone who will stop at the river's bank to
kiss you at howling,

and be blown to fragment as I am,

feeling high with something as your flutter, the buzz.

Pain is lasting, that I lost control and you went away forever,

not trusting; not seeing; not there.

The price of mistake is too high; love me?

50.
JVM

Enjoyment is in all we've done in 328 days,
driving through the sun, a stake running through the heat of joy with the
top down.
Lasting snow-storms, cold, a flurry held at bay,
romantic dinners upon layers of laughter;
Cocktails everywhere fathomed in sand, mountain or sea,
wine tasting on vineyard retreats,
Flowers bloom;
Watching naked in arms twined with lips
sun sets or rises out your bedroom;
I am calmed home, so no future known to thee,

The gas fire burns while skin heats upon night;
Animals clutch sleepily to the comfort of dream,
ocean views span priceless emotions;
Paradise nearby is innate to keep;
Hugs grip the truth while moments themselves weep,
they hold no other sometimes.

Smiles run deeper, driving the rail underneath thy heavy fluid;
Mostly the innocence of heart says stop,
about we lock safely.
Hearts kindly dance unaffected by a traverse in the wind;

Wanting trust and sincerity to lie still;
Willing to love when thinking not ever to,
to go when inclined to love without fear of breaking harder;
A *heart more* is one not loving.
The *willingness* to overt a course run;
Openness, fair to kind, and skin so rare,
opens again;
Barriers will not stand to rise.

Tears and laughter to rebuke the weather not lifting;
Snow and never cold my dear;
Summer and kisses on shoreline sands
followed by~
Life on its rise, so gather up
a chemical mix,
But what of sun, that ate the night who digested not wanting too?

Gifted to tears, yes I am,
and closeness is sadly I loom
bestowed with depth I toil on the while, imagined;
The story of two women,
the story is as expected, my end.

51.

XXYSOLMNK

If there ever was;
I knew not before
such as her.

Upon first meeting she bit and even after that.
I was then a mere visitor to her domain,
don't mess with my heart or tangle my straightened life
she demanded;

It all works without touch,
life does.
I'll draw blood again, she called from the stairway with a swipe from her
nicely sharpened claw.

I swipe at moving objects all day long,
she sang with her teeth,
a lioness in my sunny coastal California yard,
it's not Texas anymore; thanks mom!
Wind breezes yonder, because I let it so.
Do you know? The bees fear me.
I slink upon a stone path garden crouched looking for prey.
Flowers raise a cautious brow
as I prowl by their waving.
Birds stay atop taller trees.

Mice, and the neighbors too,
fear me
when I'm on the loose.

Do not think you can touch my lovely fur,
light and dark like a handmade rug,
upon a rolled over quiet nap do I show vulnerability?
Bare my soft white belly to the sun,
one eye on you or maybe two,
my sharpest yet.
Sleeping? Maybe not.
Claws pensive to strike if you're near.
I'm good.

When one winter day it all changed, the gate melted away.
The mice played at my paws,
the birds bowed to me unafraid,
those locks around my heart
dropped, busting widely spilling to the ground.
Claws didn't open when
I pressed my hand against your face,
and I didn't scratch your cheek.

My fangs stopped biting, she wonders why.
Claws stopped tearing the couch.
What's changed I asked my mom,
stay away from my heartbeat!
Soon stay away fell apart.
Who was this visitor now more than a guest?

If there ever was,
I knew not before such as her love.
A cat changed my ways in 484 days.
After all, the point was clear, that she dictated the terms for loving her.
But I pressed some affection otherwise not too much.
Now with that said of her life
she's tucked inside a cool spot on the mantel in a box,
on her terms she says goodbye to us.
Remember dear Abbey, I was there writing?
I tamed the claw without trying,
softly, gently,

a cat so brave,
beauty like no other beheld in our soulful earthy space.
A painting marked by perfect color,
bending precisely indulging one's senses of a cat with it all.

The music ended when
I touched her face for the last just afterwards.
But listening close to the stone path breeze where she remains in all of me.
In memory of Abbey, the most beautiful cat there was.
Whose presence inside my brittle body breaks me into singing;
but lives in stone in the garden with her name etched outside the kitchen
window.

52.

IN BRIGHT LIGHT

In bright light I pray
in darkness I ache
after all we are here to love forsaken,
the loss of you is more than I can take.
Wine will subdue the heart to allude it,
in reddened cloak its message; but to hide its rebuke.

As I stir Lord, I hate.
When I drink I feel love awaken,
in cloud and while fading
I beg no one!
I bow proudly.
No more to ask; No more to touch,
do not wake for what's last,
rest upon what was then,
silence be you for my body is weak;
Exasperated.
Exhaled, flatter than before
inner being deflated to the floor, and I cannot partake.

In you; your smell of sweet orgasmic releases
your hair fair and soft upon my face
your fucking hands, soft and electric, keep in custody my body.

The knowingness of your curves,
the familiarity of your shape,
I grow beholding in thy capture still.
But wrong; you said I go.
I confess to see me in peril older against yes.
I stand small in days of wonder so grand.
You can appreciate my gift,
can you not to this late hour of despair?

But I could make a list,
hence now I know, I must
remind in time this awful journey,
I let you go.

Farewell my eternity soul, twist as it is the wind in me,
uncorking the truth.
I cannot anger you because you don't know,
go forth or within whatever to eat the storm,
swallow harder to solve the weather blowing.

Except remember thee.
Remember thy nights.
Thy skin and cloud covering,
safe upon deeper moments less on others,
awakening in me,
conversations flourish past rich and deep.

You die this night,
against my body,
winged for flight,
you die a morsel of a soul, that of mine.

Bid you all thee fare thee well,
but my heart is subdued,
grown longer yet,
knows you've missed
with God's grace I will survive
the lack of you.

Point or not,
beholding to the wind falling south,
or north where I be blown,
or sun to rise as beckoned.
She runs.
She hides beyond my reach,
emptiness hath no hallway.
The wandering alone of it all,
to pace,
question when
upon soul's noose I hang!

I grasp your smell for one last rope,
holding for a time our past,
laid naked in my honest arms engulfed in seasons afterwards
is no more of course; the we.
Love has to run or be caught without her beauty,
go and go far,
stretch time and pavement heating under foot,
I am no longer your courtyard;
no bloom or garden grows,
you remain loose in spring to find ~
me, I am content behind stonewalls,
where I've lived,
where I die,
the gate is closed.
Bid you *thee* night.

53.

MORNING COFFEE

When I feel the wind climb under my limbs,
I chill as expected.
Fear rakes clearing my soul of loss,
out the door I run clinging to what?
To what was?
To perception of what could be if let?

When I feel the earth move away my wings stall in flight,
I drop.
Assumed,
forever to die,
for it's a girl I trust.
Slowly,
slowly.

I press my lips seeking under fire that burning kiss,
one open,
once again,
restore my tree,

strengthen my wings,
give me leaves green in wintertime,
flight is a beautiful thing.
A girl I am.

Less broken.
~ less dry,
~ less than,
less cracks or perfection choking at the ends.

Flight is what I seek,
to soar, not drop.
To be, not fall.

54.

VIEW FROM A CRACKED OPEN HEART

Two chairs sit empty overlooking sunlight and ripples.
Waiting to be seated,
two women journey for a hand lost,
a reason to happen suddenly among sunsets,
fumbling for words.
Reaching a travelers inn to bathe,
red mist hangs on iron weave,
weeping days grow longer.
Worried over the loss of such potent love,
oh God touch me now that I be real,
will me home or die thy only true believer!
I beg of thee to bless thy dream!
Anoint my wicked hunger,
be you; the knock at my door
fill the yard blooming; come running there; speak your heart to me,
do not waste.
It is upon happenstance that we exist.
Oh rare,
oh rare,
two chairs.

Life passing through iron howling,
waiting on new, but not to,
on us to sit.
Throttled by soft hands,
space that speaks no more.
Through weaves,
barbed wire and curves banking higher and higher,
dizzy from the drive
one fails to catch her breath in time,
bestowed with lovely to be taken once tasted,
chase the thought of it,
dashed hopes burning imbedded with wine
I remember your drink,
die for the thought of it,
two empty chairs.
Fog moves over like a season deafening sunnier days
iron is second to none in time
waiting with brine penetrating
bitter winter to some.

To fill thy seat
no one will,
for both are empty unless both filled.
Your kiss not to be succeeded
while you entertain another on the hill.
I sit in one dying, not chosen.
I will not pass without staying first,
seated says resting at the inn of within,
embraced with fire,
thy soul burdened,
dark hath no space,
I'll wander.
Sweet to me,
easy to light come take your seat
anytime.
I'm waiting to die in chair one.
But alas a pulse upon dreaming of you touching my face
falling asleep,
the possibilities; oh will wander
not landing for me, it is joy to float upon desires.

55.

STARING INTO THE THORNS OF EDEN

Its over
orange roses,
just a thorn for what was so beautiful,
a petal of what was before dying,
in flowers bloom love, but not always
for this day,
each for understanding
a laugh divides in two
for support,
staying in and hugging close,
anything to be enough for love,
this Writer bleeds,
infected
because it was a lie
someday,
somewhere.

I come ripping from this page,
hey!
Returning to fetch thy love,
thy scent,
thy capture,
thy gate,
when enough,
but when you are here,
to be,
go and go.
Run from our love
stroking myself lonely with black lace
wiping tears away,
in a drawer you left panties conveniently to remember thy presence,
scent of you,
carved in a tree, "jvm."

Never leaving again,
love when it hurts.
Love, when I can't understand.
Loving, when it looks like it, but yet another thing.
Trust, as the sand shifts,
my feet thought to be grounded take air,
trust when it takes love to be there,
when one doesn't- is rain.
Trust;
takes two or no one.
I married
not you of me.
We are Sunday mornings after making love
six minutes before the alarm
you say, "six minutes is enough,"
separation comes hard,
cannot you see the love we melted?
The lacking is less of us.
I can do no more to save,
Thus.
I turn my back.
I will love again!
I demand be free of our journey.
She will be not you!
But not; I swear…
Goodbye babycakes,
find your light in love someday.
But remember baby age burns the clock,
don't wait upon its swing.

56.

THREE DEGREES

I'm not a woman,
I am capable,
I am strong
not female at all.

I know what to do in a disaster,
know not to crawl on the roof engulfed in flames,
I know to have a wrench at the gas valve,
dangling string and all.
Not calling it "*he*" or "*guy*"!
It's a wrench please without parts!
To be a girl or a boy,
tangible objects aren't a gender,
not allowed to be a "*she?*"
What's your problem?
It!
'cause I am competent,
handyperson, not handyman,
firefighter, not fireman,
mailcarrier instead of mailman.
Please be smart. It's the title to a job!
Inclusiveness.
Words can give esteem away,
not pregnant or done with birth either,
a woman's meaning is not "waitonman,"
did you know?
Why continue to raise girls withdrawn for the kill?
Insufficient, little crippled deer,
pathetic and never brave hearted by aggression,
bound in pink and pigtails, bindings,
to more easily identify the weak sex to the hunter, as the one to take down
for a meal.
Without courage she'll run, not encounter,
hide courage and strength underneath if you are contrary to belief.
Victim instead of equalizer,
good *girl* stay quietly there!
Less than you, to be okay in the eyes of society.
Don't say no, it rocks their boat,
someone might see you strong, and take note,
don't offend stay pink! "Take back the night" but think not to offend.

How usual to be shunned for strength,
Be a woman.
To protect the status of men.
Privileged existence isn't enough for their man-sized appetite,
scratch, again. Got fleas?
Can't fuck it or
eat it with a spoon?
Kill it.
Pick it clean.
Bones out the back of the pickup truck,
guzzle her blood with canned beer.
Chase her with a hot cigarette!

57.

SAN FRANCISCO BIRTHDAY

Strings tune taut against night,
I ne'er knew hanging stars,
streets glistening pour downward into the Bay
puddle of light
oh how spilling.
It'd be life?
It'd be a cry?
It'd be joy?
A soul sputtered dry,
where loneliness strikes,
but oft to the heights

doth music play,
do the gods hear?
sounding of a single tear,
ping.

Or the *Gate* to die,
those rustic beguiling arches poised in fog, 1937,
one's answer to a question.
What is this City?
A firehouse
sleeping
a bell rings,
upon an orange dot on a panel lighting,
flashing hither,
stable doors throw open wider,
a lantern in urgency sways,
bell rings, 1906.
A gruff old Irishman stands stern, "Secure those hoses" he yells.
Engines pulled through the streets by frantic working horses with a nose for
smoke,
firelight rushes in swells,
dreams sizzle then break,
sticks succumbed by its weight,
crack like jaw.
Her blaze then rests yawning.
Her sword quieted upon rock, nothing left to strike.
I stand amid the crossing,
pages turning,
hours rip from the wall by wind
changing me.
Sweeping through vast hallways
seeking thou comfort
I am unfit.
For *thee.*
Glass and cold cement,
empty pipes rise from her eloquent complication.
Fill me
labyrinthian?
The Ferry Building, 1898,
"splendid survivor."
Thou stop suddenly, a point on our map,
Sutro Baths, 1896-1966,

"The audacity of a dreamer."
The Cliff House 1863, three times a winner.
Lillie Hitchcock Coit grabs the rope,
"Pull. You can do it!" She demands, 1851.
Knickerbockers Engine No. 5
smoke squeezes wood to idle thread,
a stump remains, but for how long?
To remembering her rich dress array of grandeur
tying her legs securely to the rocks,
resurrected by the touch of her face remembering through photographs,
the way she loved, embraced softly, the way she sweetly yearned for your
mouth.
A creak in the floorboard begs for loves past,
decking grand span waltz untouched by fervor
kisses live dying
worn to ashes
Chateau!

Obsession for the music, thirsty for a longer song,
amid tomorrows fair thee well,
Mark Twain leans upon shifting sand, 1864
Fisherman's Wharf, times changed,
Mayor Newsom defies California law, 2004
"Will you marry me?" on the steps of City Hall,
justice restored to the neighborhood!
But what is this City?
Buena Vista Café, 1952,
the Irish coffee unmistakably nectar of God's *wounds*.
Bring who you are
be not damned for difference
provide yourself.
Sail torturous Gate running the rails deep cutting her bow,
once an abstract spirit aimless,
surrender your toughest nail.
Live through adversity!
Let your wood and steel be strong!
Do not resist your knowledge
burnt to the ground- thrice.
To forget her/history is to cease upon malnutrition,
to stave the future,
is to feed the past undeserving of your banquet.

Crashing broken upon jagged edge
there, o'er
alas. •

A cautious *Muse* toils,
dancing upon your each smile
tip tap.
Energized by your beholding of her jettison beauty,
rise to her determination
fight for her life
fireworks splash the sky
radiant isn't it?
Well made in proper dimension,
raging softly within my senses,
buildings take flight in whimsical minds
bells ring in the night.
Hope too heavy grounded for a time
yet my hunger; my drive.
Hooves clack against stone
pulling carriages through North Beach.
Scoma's Pier 47, 1965
"Best chowder recipes."
Heidi released, 2006
sinking to the bottom
"I am saved!" remarked the crab,
scurrying to her depths
murky is home.
Pacific Café, 1974
Your conversation, cold, windy 34th Avenue,
laugh snuggling with strangers and wine,
hair strewn in paint colored louder,
your hand draped upon white cloth
a glint lovely against linen.

Hang tight thy sails
when the mast shifts
the end doesn't exist,
we are always beginning
as told by Ocean Beach,
and her majesty
our will.

58.

DEAR MS. CLIPPERS

I missed the point you can see through dense glass,
you know everything,
but we remain a closed window.
You keep us from developing into whatever if anything we are meant to be,
by blocking these hearts raining to assume the worst like your past.
But seasons change,
do they not? Winter cold becomes summer's warmth?
I feel like a clipped tree limb once strong and brave,
cut back after growing too close to your transom.
Closer my limbs grew,
outstretching of my leaves,
your powerful love nurtured my growth,
why?
Like sun and water built my reaching,
then, when I sprout openly with waking exuberance further still,
your sharpened tools fly from the shed.
Damn you, nearer my heart!
Cut my branch sawing, killing my touching,
alone reaching still, I am recoiled home,
severed,
cut off,
but you'll never forget me,
love holds that.

59.

TOP OF SATURN

Your body
slips over my skin
boiling hot, and embers glowing,
my mouth on your breast comes to mine
heart piercing.
Force to take.

Lips touch the ache
bleeding me please.
Quiet forest thickens
rich like oil
simple as earth
everyday my joy to breathe.

If sun rises upon wet
flowers bloom
park benches empty ask to let
forever your touch inside my beaming
watching through window.
Peering through glass,
see me, love me; as I you,
even you; defects refine in mine
rich like the sea
kisses filled with salt,
warm temperatures fuck on the horizon.

Land succumbs to sky in making love,
riding the wave for them.
I'll wait upon thee ~ to be my bride.
Your body
smooth like shell ears
beckons my trust
asking so.
Shape moves within
moves without
my fingers feel the way
across

porcelain white sand
to hazel blue sea,
I rinse.
Lie still,
in morning
as I part in half.
Split from the tree,
falling,
endless,
beginning,
drop,
landing,
softness.
Dust flings.

60.

LUXOR

Firewater for the heart, kisses wet and smooth like paper.
Just a girl for love
pissed off.
Addicted to the fluids, the skin too.
Enjoyed the last taste,
drank too much of you.

61.

FEELING, DYING, TRYING

The marker for dying is pain;
the marker for living is love
and being alive to tell of it.
Resistance to self is death always,
who is that be known until grave,
the marker for doing is fear
and fear be evil,
sip from its cup
perish.
For fire burns brightly hither there,
roads tempt between sufferings,
searching one's soul,
taunting with innocence,
if it be bleeding, sick or infected.
Life hung low
do cauterize.
Searing on each side evenly
lost in the inequities of life
overdone.
Clock outweighs the sun
no hands to touch
no fingers to scroll
no eyes to see thy *beauty*
no legs to seek our path,
blinded by eyes burned shut,
peeking is pain
seeing who are they,
before death.
But too near to try,
the calling stabs at restlessness and to order is unattainable.
Repeating until one submits to its inner ringing.
Hear that thunder
fists swing at air
in fight of it,
can't stop.
Can't ignore.
Beginning to grasp thy tormented existence,
operating from emotional damage.

62.

WHEN LOVE KILLS

A heart,
it will grow most anywhere,
where it is safe
where it is kind
trusted and sure,
spreading its vines.

To pick the right soil to attempt us.
I picked a rock on a hillside once and couldn't root,
instead of admitting it,
I didn't give up.
I kept struggling to find a way through stone,
to nestle my seed.
Aromatic where seeking residence
a wet redwood nest, a spot in the sun that spreads through thick tree
branch,
leeching.
In every crack, I gained momentum;
But no place to seed,
I got comfortable thinking to stay,

I saw ground,
it was rock,
I saw sun ~ it rained.
I saw love,
it was not.
So you said,
so you were wrong,
finding soil is what I finally did and you, to *stone*.

63.

REVELATION

I'm not crazy,
reacting crazy to you.
Drawn insanity running from my pores scared to death.
Loving me like no other then by a day's dawning perplexing surgery.
Remove what beats, ripping nails out of wet wood.
The fission between
what lives embraced,
what *pulses* below our lunar surface,
another lover then another,

I burn; they burn,
she'll burn.
I am not jealous,
you lose~ no one wins
in this *game.*

You've trashed me so grin upon your hearty work.
Stand in line your next victim of deception,
she be unsuspecting, as I,
blonde and blue cruelty.
I called you *Beauty.*
Certainly unusual
looking at someone who doesn't deal with anything uncomfortable.
Used me; use them, and that one.
Lies pelted upon my life, stoning my affection.
Soft kisses sped upon hell's slick track,
banking mercifully left, then right.
You said, "just a girl."
I came, screaming joy,
you lied.

64.

PUT "P" BACK IN LESBIAN

The stoning of rich women,
tirade of dinner conversations,
rage and anger.
It's rich people's fault;
the war,
the poor,
my bank account,
global warming gone cold,
holes unexplained in the Universe,
smoking cars,
feminism,
diaper rash,
on this isle we do whine.
You man-hater, shouted over plates shifting across bloody hillside lace cloth.
If equal rights is your preferred fare?

One shouts pausing with one eye to the wall.
What kind of female are you anyway?
Questions attacking, shooting aspire,
not self-mutilating or self-deprecating?
My God?
Not weak like me?
Not glass thinner to shatter.
You're confident, so why be different?
I forgot the question!
Oh dear, you will spoil the well spreading your brave poison,
this I know well fed.
How dare you display your courage and strength among family,
in my face where I can see your mighty armor flex.
Women are victims by choice,
can't you remember this?
Stay the course, of which.
Politics prattle, "it's everyone else's fault."
Blab on another rib, spread fodder,
no matter the price,
I am right!
My way is all there is.
Be me, not you, so I can reconcile my choices,
goulash is pouring over your plate
damn you.
We're going to have a lynching
for dessert.
Third world country now,
wasn't once,
other views not allowed except just one,
the ship's run aground stopping dead.
Women who hate women for difference sake;
lesbians sleep with women,
heterosexual women sleeping with men,
I'm not straight like you,
not assimilating into hetero vilified,
where differences are eliminated,
to be the same is no more me!
I'm a lesbian.
Another species of human, see the television.
I am a lesbian like me and to care about you.
We are the same in love and pain, same for our loss and freedoms.

65.

LOOKING DOWN THE BARREL

This day of firearms laid to ground,
our first meeting since that other time,
of war,
guns drawn,
of defeat and bitterness,
no trust or belief anymore in what we had,
our love like the leaf unexplained,
taken by the wind scattered about
a miracle, the tree.

Life budding where one cannot fathom it would root
how we became to this earth deeply
when chance was fortune once.
Purpose was thy bedding,
veins suckled on morning to survive.
Knowingly we drank upon
your skin wet under my fingers
tips hungrily read out loud searching, drawing your pores into my mouth.

What became of us in the end will tell today,
like rings in a tree about age.
Not sure about friends,
my nerves are tight—pulsing even, shooting wide firing inside the walls of
my chest,
I glance at the clock
pending *that* dong by mallet
Will I be strong?
Confident not crumble or cry
at the base of her stature,
will all the strength I've learned fall away,
at sight of you.
At kisses you'll faithfully give,
meaning only friends.
Remembering our passions before rocks hit
without you in bed.
I drift, but not slept since.
I'm supposed to know today and thought I did,
empty again that I wasn't more brave
someone else touches your lips Sunday mornings.
I can't bear the thought.

I'm not ready yet!
I cannot see you
I will break,
I'm sure.
I fear tumbling through dark airless space,
I'm not crazy.
Spinning out of comfort now,
pick up the phone; say not today,
not ever again,
cannot bear the pain,
yet coffee cannot hurt,
breakfast can't crack a wound rage,
seeing you across the table in Tiburon cannot be my demise twice,
just toast and eggs with a small orange juice,
can't hurt,
didn't back when,
I must know.
It's looking into your bluest eyes afloat on a raft,
I miss me adrift in *thy* sea.

Sun rising over burning orange with aqua cresting,
carrying my heart bobbing,
nothing but space to design a different 'morrow,
only water and deeper pride,
the future out there asking what if.
What if my love was enough?
What if?
You could love me.
You could open wide like that yonder ocean,
like me spread beholding,
under water quiet and surreal,
now pacing at the clock anxiety between times.
Waiting sick to annoy its calling with ticking,
start the car and drive to you as fast as the roadster will go.
Turning into the lot to die on the wheel.
Will you show for our meeting after so long, still afraid of us?
Will you hate me still,
because you loved?
Will you ever know who I am without distortion?
What we mean together despite the past and how we define our love; *rarely.*
And will again keep coming back in lovers next.
Your face appears fresh raw like it were yesterday,
oh Time I hate you!
Trusting now you are whom I think you are,
emotionally dangerous.
Am I crazy?
Growing from rock after months of bleeding sap,
sprouting still in love with you
I grew.
Not you folded inside the lockdown,
silent in your head
peace upon your future inevitably to have more love despair.

66.

EROSION

Where earth fights not to be lost
gripping at edge,
fingers grasp at a crack or corner to hold at tips

slipping without means to stop a stampede,
the weight of your leaving
abandonment, rejection, betrayal, silence,
breakdown.
Face tarred unresponsive to light
invisible over time or transported,
reduced to no matter at all
destroyed to never was
or worse, to fog.
Reaching through agony still searching seeing light
momentum
release,
you appear in dream from behind the Red Door.

Impossible
insane
to believe.
You're the one for mornings lingering past the alarm.
My one sand; my one soul print in creation,
dumped, ravaged and killed to death,
wounds flying
once steel now foil,
so quick rushing to someone else
to destroy what was growing
birthed to *Us.*

Fighting until nothing but our hearts are left.
The bloody battle not to love,
broken to love; our once again oneness,
bronco's busted to a quiet dawn incubating under covered heat.
Pacing slowly to the noses
soft and supple
strong and stable,
the scent of you cauterized to memory
the changed.
For keeping faith, I lie safe with you now
not insane visible all the while
never to be another or another or another
dust settled.
We killed the avoidance of truth
we submitted to home exhausted

rising claim to our music
our destiny to song
you are forgiven in this life and our next
yet conditioned upon earth living
and your holding me as your lover.

67.

PINK DRESS

New York for winter
snows deeper eclipsed
slick fog creeping down wetting streets
my mouth lay open wide to hear you breathe.
My fantasy to touch would not happen then or I knew ever
you walked from dream overtaking me,
could I chance to love, to fall so hard?
Forced to walk the cold stair for soft and fluffy,
best to be lovers with short range hearts,

my best opinion yet.
I've got it now by months of trying
almost three years of dying
of pounding,
of desire,
of mouths shivering open, feeding wildly,
hungry for pink
of weary tears soaking my *French* tuxedo.

Suddenly you appeared last place I expected.
On Highway One near the *Golden Gate* where I jumped feet first
against my wanting to live!
I plead standing romantically at vertigo edge
smacking my head.
Cold, drowning, remembering your faded warmth,
if it was ever not imagined,
fighting the current, soon would pull me under.
Why again this suicide?
Attracted to the fall?
The Bridge strung her web in bloody iron,
the end of feeling?
Your returned love of mere efforts to soften guilt
too many remains are abandoned unanswered or worked.
You leave better than stay.
Abandon better than tie the knot.
Quit rather than sweat the annoyances of touch
remain rusty instead.

Heavy early morning runs frightened streaming from my pores
looking for an open doorway to heaven or hell.
Banging to get out, but not wanting to.
An echo returns my pain
you cried in my arms waiting, begging me to your bed.
I was happy you're gone.
Let me go I begged upon your continued ovation.
Called the demons; Rid me of this infliction to love one that cannot love me!
Tormented soaking wet
snow sticking to my face,
car lights flash opening like a Universal lens,
wider reaching devouring slowly chewing me.
The ideal picture of two madly always twisted flakes in love.

Can't pull away
melting!
Wider the aperture
bigger your bite,
wrenching at loss once mine passed.

Shoulders pressed against the window
shall I?
Resist the rail,
no, I won't go; I pulled back,
dizzy by the long way down
looking *yonder.*
Red paint concealed my palms
where was I caught this time?
Beauty, physically, shiney like anchovy
blonde like Miami
flamingo feathers ruffling in the warm sun
I taste pink driving my car.
Walking in my neighborhood
smelling Redwoods scented by shade,
pink in the middle of a meeting.
Feathers *coo* to intersect upon my skin.
Sitting in the back of a taxi
it's pink!
So back to the Bridge,
to die
to cry
to live.
Gamble with… my mind.
Cable cars and fog; running across Market Street
last time I saw you,
crying with my soul emptying slowly into vast spaces
my palms redder.
Gripping decisions
paint or blood.
Do I jump?
Or somewhere else
the pink dress.
Pencil writing thinner and thinner words,
scribble runs fading from legibility.
Like paper the night screaming, graphite the hunted.

No message this time
not another kiss to be,
the quiet of over.
Our mouths never will again,
subtle of snow drifts into the fire
settled on incompatibility!
The reason why
love doesn't matter after all
to the few of you who lose.

68.

UNIVERSE

I follow the path of death
one trail after another
emotional boulders too heavy to lift,
to carry,
to shovel,
to push,
tis' life.
Quarry at five a.m.,
nothing moved by five
nothing moved in years,
push and lift.
Nothing's changed just more hard working,
not a hole is dug,
not a rock disappeared,
not a ground penetrated,
no path opened.
Hard as hard is…
Cannot stop the survival of moving things not budging.
My power wanes,
my strength weakens.
My dreams are too rich to think.
How to release my unlived life inside?
If I had a day, maybe three to be that,
instead I'd plow,
instead I'd slave.

I endure a life of tribulation working against my desires,
my purpose.
My loss deteriorates my life soul,
my cable to receive,
and dying my gifts to those,
who I am nothing to survival,
the poor die first scrapping at fortune breaking,
let me go
let it be my glass
my chance
my living,
my intended lived life transforming,
gun shot fire sudden,
through wall it hovers dancing
picking its target.
Me, it hovers over thinking,
I die ~ *you.*
Someone else die,
what's the worth?
Nothing.
What's my problem?
I never was!
Until this.

69.

TURN A BAD PENNY

You've come into my life
sounds corny to say,
you're looking at your butch,
from across the sea.
With your intellectual smile, sensuality, and cautious-thinking,
where distance is relative.
I stood not far away,
something clicked between us.
A romance then kindled,
on a night after a long day, that one that loomed,
I left to answer another call,

I had to go back to touch the *end,*
you knew this.
You loved me anyway.
As her heart betrayed me numerously,
after passionate manipulative kisses,
faking loving me.
Or betraying her deep love for me?
Whom?
She returned to her "x" perfectly sounding,
in bed with me,
emotional rejection of the devastating kind *first* came.
One with money,
a clean car,
one who is less risk.
Monotone, not a writer conflicted with words.
Cyclist came the storm, relentless,
stirring up my foundation
spinning my head.
Picking up my home flinging it skywards,
and you call *me* being angry.   .
I say, "I didn't mean to hurt you."
I'm done with her, the other femme in the other roadster.
I exclaimed pleading from my heart,
loving two fabulous women
except one a *bad penny.*
One will take me and I her,
not to look back.
Upon clearing of a storm's debris
let down hard from the *sky.*
I am one butch landing,
one *boi* and one woman inside.
It's your love that I belong.
Scriptwriting on Sunday mornings,
movies watched in dim light,
last night at a LA hotel on your business trip.
Making love as you call it
while I say, "sex now please!"
Making home
faithful,
not betraying.
Kissing that never lies,

but connects truth deep within,
supportive during sun or piercing rain.
Integrity,
ethic.
My femme looking out after me,
I'll have your back she says,
never letting a knife enter unexpectedly.
My hand as quick as my suspecting eye,
when you slip,
I'll not walk over you to keep my hands upright
or my life *unruffled.*
Stoked warm not grey smolder.
Have it all!
Why not?
And there's more,
growing making two less brilliant into one more exquisite.
I should not have gone back to quit,
I knew she hadn't changed,
acceptance ~
honor.
Open doors to take your bags,
feed the dog and not forget the cat.
Love in an unloving world,
more concerned with pollution
electric cars; note the price!
or where to dump trash.
Come back from recycling, to love.

70.

ROCK AND HARD WITH LOVE

From my perspective,
we cannot live in peace with anger,
we cannot live with each other,
leaving when there's work,
self-absorbed, stuck on oneself,
a fight or disagreement,
you run for the palm.
"Incompatibility," heard it again!
With just me or?
Or is doing the work necessary between lovers,
whatever lover you pick she will feel the wall.
Beyond an affair is to submit.
Will you find her?
The one who's perfect for your mitten,
the right fit, the same every day.
Consistent to death until do you part,
always healthy,
not even a cold,

doesn't talk like you,
who is rich with money,
who doesn't live by poorly selling words facing a grim market.
But linear thinking, that's the one!
Emotion squeezed slow from the tube.
Yet filled only by our love,
changing lovers to avoid it's you!
Intimacy is rich
a coin, a cage without love,
filling me drawn from a faucet
when lucky enough to find it, overflow,
stopping short at the hurdle,
stalled on a dime.
Every time,
won't jump over
just do it!
Sadly,
the other side was safe
you couldn't see.
No vision of what was in front
all you wanted in one.
Loving, successful and supportive.
You, damaged by the past
I couldn't fix,
only love does after submitting to its existence
like the sun rising,
beauty.

Dance because it is there to behold
reaching so far
boring than taming the wild,
not understanding that the wild goes for home
and wild fizzles for *the one.*
Settling where the fire keeps burning
hot that will never cool,
I reached inside you soaking the bed.
Waiting on you when you worked so hard,
I learned to cook damn you!
Sucked up but not returned,
checkmate was near.
"Incompatibility."

If I hear one more chime of it!
Switching bodies
to rid yourself of me.
Your heart will never free,
you have stopped for less in the cage you avoided.
But you've got one with money
stoic, uneventful, steady I am sure.
I ended up with more!
It is you who doesn't get it!

71.

MERRY CHRISTMAS, 2006

Invested so little in wrapping
as little as possible.
Tying that special bow
in paper and ribbon
compared to what's given.
Fear changed the course
even tree lights burned brightly,
yet failed to respond.
Cheating your true one lover
I misread your intentions,
got caught in the heat.
Not interested you hear
but so far.
In you, any time of year, then,
why pull me back into your arms,
attachment disorder avoids the need for clean-up,
remaining in control of feelings
able to start and stop with a shift of mood.
How does someone keep so clean in love?
Dial is preset, that's it!
Even knowing how close to get
not very, everything moves but not.

72.

WORDSMITH

Writing doesn't come from where I am today,
but from where I've been.
There is no tomorrow or now in my life
only yesterday.

Writing is to catch up,
so I can cope with the future I cannot stop.
The present if ever seen; lives starving on high hopes.
Positive affirmations and dreaming,
mostly based on the attainment of losing.

73.

ACCELERATIONS

You say you love me,
tears run screaming on your face
filling up time.
You're in love with me.
But don't want me,
I finally heard the loud pushing away loving alone hears.
Go to her, that you will love her enough someday,
as I fade,
I must.
You know go now to live my life, that intended one you were a part of,
the one you shuddered from, the one I am mostly.
She is who you want so do what it takes to marry her.
Goodbye is my response from the tears we've both cried,
three times the charm as said in the literature.
Too much hurt my dear thou committed by your hand.
You closed every door I opened,
locked every gate quicker than I arrived to peer over into the lovely garden
on warmer days,

the smell of earth mixed with the morning sun knocked loose the clouds.
Who owns that land I'd ask?
Not me I'd reply, peering.
I'm trespassing.
You have no right to come to me now with your gift of leaky heart.
As much as I look to touch at it's quaking held in my hand.
The one that could've been Christmas or Valentine's Day lying in a red box.

74.

FROM THE FRYING PAN TO LOVE

Words stir like rue,
heating over a stovetop,
sometimes overheating in the iron skillet
working to make sense.
Ease the fire down and stir again.
By degree becoming thicker and more tasty,
keep stirring adding more support,
and more butter because of color,
never, never walk away.
It's the constant attention that makes gravy,
poured over hot home baked biscuits makes breakfast.

75.

LOVE ME WHEN IT IS

Love me like I am,
love me who,
for that which is.
Love me no matter how long,
but for now!
Because I upright a fallen drunk,
live with integrity, not ever to waiver,
no shortcuts or human ladders,
don't wait until I marry you, it's the interconnectedness
we have today.
Love me because we lost so many years to toast our special life,
reach in the night for I desire soul.
Hit by the sad rock!
Discouragement grips with a fist holding me, not rejecting or withholding
support,
love me because I've earned that status by deeply loving you.
My being there when the mud slid,
don't wait until I am more than I am or when I am your vision of me,
it's then too late.
Build the road as we travel forward, not that is finished ahead.
the earth is flat at the edge,
"okay what's next?"
Throw out another street we create by candlelight,
pencil and pen drawing with a common thread,
by dimmer light, colder, heavy rain collecting plink in hope's gutters.
Care about everyone you are in contact with, that they gain by your
interaction,
we are connected by our hunger, thirst and united pain.
The *ultimare*, if you don't do; then I am not.
Don't love me 'cause I am gone.
Care about my life struck with a tear or two,
feel me break and glue pieces when you can,
don't say I'll do and don't move,
love me for what I deserve.
What I earned after my time was swallowed whole,
gulped and chomped.
Standing upon a torrid - eagerly devouring shore stronger
defeating harsh winds shoving my back, waves pawing me to death
drawn to die; but lived.

76.

AFTER YOU'RE GONE WHAT THEN

Looking back no pictures exist,
I am erased.
Not a child, not a red tricycle, no skinned knee to remember me.
Except this morning, a broken guitar in mind represents my memory.
It was missing strings, a life of growing up that's deleted.
White wood guts strenuously splattered upon a dark wood floor,
blood of trees, an oriental carpet,
a violent awakening to who I was then,
nothing more past to trace who I've become,
not remembering.
Was an accident that took *that* me away.
How now to reconcile this body grown up?
My abandonment issues, running away from love, scared to pieces like
shattered wood.
My pain?
The music quakes as to thunder.
New lovers waking upon sweet "like to get to know you" conversation,
who are you she asks covered by satin sheet.
That looming question sends me running curiously to search.
I can't say who I was.
"It doesn't appear upon my calling,"
I tell,
just dark; blankness, and sad. I am.
I wonder. Curious, who?

A car accident ravaged *her* life away from these young hands,
I no longer in a flash of red ambulance lights had a chance.
Died at seventeen with vibrant dreams going down to the river.
Three minutes later, a pulse *she's* alive,
I'm not leaving!
My crazy *wicked* brothers say you're lucky you don't remember our
childhood!
"Look at us?" I do see psychotic, sociopath, worthless to those most needing
more of them.
Should I be glad then I don't remember where I lived, what friend I favored,
or what dog slept at the foot of my Apple Wood bed?

Then should I be glad I don't remember who I wanted to be all grown up?
What's my purpose?
Am I there yet?
Will I know when I get there?
Sparks of memory jump like lights dangling from the roof blinking in the
rain.
I couldn't talk or walk,
broke glass to speak,
the victim of traumatic brain injury, so young to end,
however old to begin again, before the survivor,
before my being here.
The biggest responsibility is to remanufacture the self-soul.
Am I glad I lived?
Don't know yet,
Rodney died instead of me.
Am I glad I lived instead of him?
Not yet.
Should've been me crumpled up inside that roadster flesh tumbling on fire.
Rolling July, summer rolling, spinning warm days, flipping over and over.
Then the quiet asphalt quenched its thirst,
after the car exploded on my blood.
A silent dusk meeting with fate,
siren's and crowds converged like a bake-off parade.
One onlooker said, shaking his head, "Just children. A real shame."
The charred bones of one,
burned, broken, dead on arrival of the other.
Star in the sky got one eye picked below.
Later a moon rose back arched upon crickets calling from that road's taking.
Saluting James Dean who died there before us,
on Highway 46.
Tumbleweeds hurriedly crossed the street,
skipping toward a safe open field,
my skull cracked,
my brain bleed swollen,
my body burned,
my eyes couldn't see blindly.
Where was mommy?
On her way crying,
maybe this is why I'll never grow up?
You asked that too,
always be that child at seventeen, 'cause I lost it when it came my turn.

But heck, my spirit never burned or changed, that is what's of me.
The romance part of my brain took me a drift.
Light on a journey to discover myself over the tormented years,
that day was hot or the orange was sweet,
laughing while juice runs from my mouth,
the changed to and changing from, seeking *the* who is you.
Telling my story while taking another bite,
so that is it, my new lover‐ getting to know me.
My will is to survive, to say I lived.
Cholame, California.

77.

LIGHTS OUT

Your special cream in the frig,
your goat cheese,
crackers lie alone in the cabinet,
your scent.
You're preset selectively,
waiting at the door,
knock.
It doesn't come.

Knowing you're gone,
I fade, to not
after so long trying
I left you.
Kicking and screaming
cold then hot.
Whatever channel
turn, turn, turn
click.

Loved me like no other could,
yet leave for one wrong thing,
a small thing.
Saying how displeased
how I live my life mostly
forgetting all the rest of the sky.

The taste between our thighs,
crystallized, shine,
forgetting the love, the passion,
to summarize, one wrong thing displeasing you,
betrayal comes in all ways to harm what's right.
You cheat of mind and heart,
don't work anything through,
don't tell the truth
clear the trouble
sweep the porch
walk away.

78.

HEART INTEGRITY

A heart shall leave (whimpering to the door) without its
nurturing by the one who planted it.
Or those hired to tend her,
living honestly by the planter's kindness to find good soil, two.

Live, to rivet her softness
a suckling heart.
Vulnerable as a puppy with tail wagging upon her big eyes upon you,
a young lamb forever dependent,
a heart fragile and attached for breathing
trusting and sweet.
Never would you take a hammer to a lamb
or cut through a puppy.
Why slam a heart
that someone's entrusted?

Heart integrity is the "*one*,"
that earth; that moves when she enters the room,
the rumbling chocking desires landscaped and painted 'yonder,
except there are many "*ones*"
no despair
gladly.
Just meeting the match to connect its fire ready to sizzle
two halves of something most valuable
a warm blanket,
emotional intelligence
the dirt where it grows
circulating to breathe her first breath
Marilyn Monroe.
Betrayal, a sad disease of the heart
things forced upon a wanting of,
walks the dishonor
love, the oxygen.
Blood, the reason, the river is running
glue to stick
cells define
the clock tied to time.
The intersection to catch her like a bus,
but:
Where *wife*, is what results.

About the Author

Tyler Stanley is a freelance scriptwriter, novelist and poet. She is a member of the Redwood Writer's Chapter of the California Writers Club, and has been published in four editions of its writers' anthology, *Vintage Voices*. She also authored *Ballad of an Imagined Woman*, published in *A Women's Anthology*, and her work *San Francisco Birthday* was selected for publication in *Bridges: A San Francisco Writers' Conference Anthology*. Ms. Stanley is currently working on a murder-romance screenplay, and has written three novels, including *Churning the Red Earth*, a nonfiction account of surviving traumatic brain injury.

Printed in the United States
131304LV00004B/211-309/P

9 780595 482504